36
YEARS *of*
SOLITUDE

*Writings from
Prison and Beyond*

ANTONIO SINOHUI SANCHEZ

ISBN: 979-8999183507

Produced by Publish Pros | publishpros.com

This book is dedicated to my parents, Josephine Sinohui and Eduardo Sanchez, who never saw the bad in me. RIP.

To my "Zoom family," who have always encouraged me to follow my dream and write: Dahlia Aguilar, Kay Cordtz, Susan Hutchinson, Jan Marquart, Mario Montoya, Sue Moore, Ivy Raff, Camille Taiara, and Leslie Webster.

And a special thanks to El Maestro Jimmy Santiago Baca.

The Great Spirit
has never left me alone
on my journey
to unravel my existence
and purpose on
Mother Earth

CONTENTS

FOREWORD

Antonio is a very special man, a memoirist and poet, in good physical condition, working with his hands and back as he does, an elder with a generous heart and indefatigable spirit. How he maintained his integrity over decades in prison, and how he could write such spellbinding prose and poetry, still puzzles me.

I met him when he attended my annual JSB Writing Retreat. When I learned he drove from California to New Mexico to attend, I was impressed. When I learned of his past, I was nothing short of amazed by this man with graying hair and a smile to melt the Arctic. In his prime, he must have been a formidable adversary and an unrivaled friend.

We became friends, and he showed me his work. The sentences were clear and precise, emotionally true, nothing facile here. It was good enough to be published, and I told him so. I even reached out to a publisher I knew, asking him to publish Antonio's work.

So as not to take up more space and time, and to let the reader see and hear and feel for themselves how beautiful Antonio's work is, I'll end here.

Jimmy Santiago Baca
Award-winning poet, screenwriter, actor, producer

AUTHOR'S NOTE

Every writer has a story; every story needs an audience. Our thoughts apply meaning to life that can help other people deal with life situations or look at them from a different perspective. The value of words and the impact they have on society or individuals can never be weighed on a scale. Each person takes a word, a sentence, a paragraph and interprets it their own way—some positive, some negative. The key is getting the mind working and taking a different approach to the words being read.

I have gone through a very troubling youth. It seemed normal when I was growing up; only as an adult am I able to understand that it wasn't. I was smoking by fourteen; I was an alcoholic and addicted to drugs before I turned twenty. My lifestyle and the people I chose to hang out with led me to being incarcerated.

Growing up in Escondido, California, in 1960 was confusing as a Mexican. At home we ate and loved our food: frijoles, arroz, tortillas—all the ingredients needed to make burritos for lunch. In elementary school, we were made to feel ashamed by the Americans for not eating ham and cheese sandwiches for lunch.

A lot of us started to question our own race. Who were we? Where did we fit in? I'm Mexican/Indian, a race that wasn't accepted in Escondido from 1960 up until I got arrested in July of 1980. At Central Elementary School, we weren't allowed to speak Spanish during school. I wasn't allowed to use my given name—Antonio—at school; it was too Mexican, so they switched it to "Tony" without my mom's permission.

A lot changed in the thirty-six years I was incarcerated; Escondido has plenty of Mexican restaurants now, and our language is spoken in most establishments. People line up to eat Mexican food, take burritos for lunch, listen to our music, and they deny they were ever against our existence.

These poems were written at different stages of my life and are a reflection of my past, present, and sometimes, future. When I was young and didn't know who I was or where I was going, I never imagined prison was going to be part of my plans in life, but it gave me the opportunity to grow and make sense of my life today.

Making the wrong choices in prison can lead to unspeakable consequences. I don't know how I survived being incarcerated for over thirty-six years in the California penitentiary. There were days when I felt hopeless and wanted to quit on myself, but I knew that loneliness is a drug best left alone.

I hear the parakeets awakening in our cozy apartment. There is a light mist cascading down the sliding door, and I am instantly taken back to Deuel Vocational Institution and administration segregation, K-Wing. I had no television or radio, the only thing that would keep me sane were the birds that were able to find their way inside and keep me company without committing a crime.

I have been out of prison for eight years, and the memories will be with me forever, a constant reminder of where I never want to be again!

Being released from prison was nothing like a movie. I had a life sentence and decades to think about my past, present, and future.

Writing has always helped me deal with my emotions. I'm able to understand what I am going through with greater clarity.

The first section, "Impulse," includes poems written while I was incarcerated. They were written about how I viewed my situation, reminders of what couldn't be spoken about and thoughts that were best kept to oneself.

"Making Amends" is the most difficult writing I have ever done. It is a self-examination based on the twelve steps of Alcoholics Anonymous and its virtues. Admitting there was something wrong with my character and the way I treated other people was very difficult for me. Being accountable for the person I was and the emotional and physical abuse I was responsible for was integral to my being released by the parole board. Every person in the California penitentiary sentenced to life has to have a parole board hearing to attain their freedom.

"Everydayness" is how I perceive the world. Writing in the present with thoughts that I try to separate prison thoughts from is challenging. You can never escape your memories. The places I have been, the things I have seen, somehow these different times coexist in the present and help me think about the future—my future of giving back to society and helping those in need.

PHASE 1

IMPULSE

RESIDENCE

We were kids… Mexicans
Growing up in the city
Raza… Third generation
My kids… Kids… Are the fifth

Beaners… Wetbacks… Chicanos
The Americans used
Derogatory words… To describe us
We watched… Each other's back
As we roamed the streets
Before the Barrio… Was created

We tattooed our city's name
On our body… Like a coat of arms
Yes… Chicano… I'm a soldier
Protector… Of my gente… Raza

The new generation
They moved into the city
Live only… In a small section
Like the Americans… Before them
They use derogatory words
Against the Raza
Forget the golden rule
To divide… Is to be… Conquered…….

EMULATE

It's Sunday morning
And I really should... Be at church
But instead... I'm outside
Looking at the sun... Building energy

We're living under... The Fifth Sun
We have resurrected Nahuatl
As our language... Tattooed our bodies
With ancient shields... Pyramids
Dream of being a warrior... In theory only

It's too early to go outside
Warriors that dream
They stay concealed... Under the covers
Are told how to act... And I realize
The times have changed
As I squint at the sun

I'm at church... Outside
In the clear sky... The sun speaks to me
Tells me the story... Of the Old Ones
And how they lost their way

Knowledge was their fruit of wisdom
Wisdom was the bearer of consciousness
Consciousness was the home of decisions
Decisions were their instrument
Of destruction.......

SUICIDE

I drink alone
No one hears my thoughts
I hate everything... Even myself
I accept my fate... To perish
And be discovered... As a relic

Maybe they will write a story about me
How in a fit of rage I destroyed a kingdom
With only one sword that was forged
By the Ancient Elders... From metal that was unknown

For a day... Week... Month
I bought into the concept
That I could be reborn
And my life had purpose
Where I was able to correct the past

And then... Who was I kidding
I was born to see this... To the bitter end
And it is much more acceptable... To my being
When I see life... With eyes closed
And hear what I want to hear

In the life I created of myself
I drink alone... Not to escape my past
But to deal with the present... Future
Where I'm always the hero... Of my saga.......

DEMORALIZED

I was born... Mexican
My family was from Mejico
I wore basketball shoes from K-Mart
And ate beans and rice wrapped in tortillas

I spoke Eng-Mex... Before bilingual
I didn't know who I was
And my parents... Couldn't
Answer my questions... Of existence

I lived in shame
Hid my identity... With violence
I wanted to be an American
But my skin was brown

I found solitude... In prison
My escape from society... Assimilation
I spoke from my heart... To find peace

I'm not ashamed of my
K-Mart basketball shoes
I'm Mejicano... My existence...
Is unknown.......

MISTRESS

In the Pinta
I eat alone
Watch everything
Listen to myself

I gaze at the sunset
Behind barbed wire
And concrete structures
Waiting for the night

In the Pinta... Mija
You're my only friend
The love of my life
As I count stars
That appear out of the dark

Each day that I awake
The Pinta is my foe
It wants me to stay forever
Never wanting me to know
The love of my life.......

SENESCENT

I saw the buzzards hovering above me
Do they know that I'm a walking dead?
Can they see the crevices that engrave my face?
Or are they blinded by their reflections
That emanate from my hairless scalp?

The calendar is my oracle of the future
Or the past... Whichever life is available
I didn't know that I was primitive... A fossil
Until I was reminded... By youth

Isolated with only memories
My last friend that sometimes evades... Me
Keeps me laughing to myself
We were born as twins... My shadow

I look as young... As I always have
If I don't look in the mirror
I don't see the crevices
That harvest the memories... That I have sowed.......

RAZA

I'm a Chicano
Living in America
I drink tequila
And eat tacos

I don't know history
I was educated
In the USA
That reminds me
Of Tijuana

I'm bilingual
Sort of
I never mastered
Any language

That's why... I'm Chicano
Derogatory being
Stuck between two worlds
Searching for my... Identity.......

SULLEN

Help me find my way back
I took a different route
To explore the other spectrum
A kaleidoscope of thoughts

Now I can't even think
I'm stuck without purpose
Waiting for a new day... To begin
If this one... Would ever end

I walk in circles
Think in metaphors
As my savior dissolves
In the coolness of water

I'm not sick... Anymore
I found my way back
With the early morning sermon
But now... Two days later
I can't move... Or talk

I shut my eyes... Play possum
So the world... Disappears
And I fight this battle... In my mind
Until... I find my way back... To purpose.......

FOLSOM

Morning is when it starts
Sounds of awakening
Life begins at dawn
People become the other

Sleepless with dreams
Spirits trap the weak
Drive them insane
Voices from death

You live someone else's nightmare
Violence directs you
Fear of sleeping too late
There is no peace... In here

Blood dripped from a fresh blade
Footsteps were heard down the corridor
No face was seen passing by
And the wind cradled
Her new child

Morning is what you become
At night the dreams... Begin
Hatred stirs the spirits
Stone... Concrete... Steel
Are caressed by inmates
As convicts remember
From isolation... The war.......

LA VISITA

I spit shine my shoes
Think of you... Mi Amor
As I wait for tomorrow
La dia... De visitas

I crease my shirt
Do my tramados
They are sharp
Like a vato... Loco

Shower and shave
Every hair in place
I drink coffee
Listen... For my name

In the visita
I look at you... Mi Amor
I don't want the day... To end
And my heart stays... On your lips
As we kiss... And I see you
Walk away... From this.......

OUTAGE

The walls... Are starting to talk to me
And people don't hear me... Anymore
I'm benevolent... My last act... Will be self-induced
I will fly like the premature birds
That fall to their death

I will paint the concrete... Crimson
People will stare in awe
Chess pieces won't move
Cards won't be shuffled

The last sound that I will hear... Is laughter
Fish will always be fish
And donkeys will always be complete... Donkeys
The concrete is approaching and reality... Disappears
The authority... Awakens

I talk to my new friend
The wall just keeps the cold out... Now
I see a man in a white suit
He looks weary and old
I stay in my fetal position
Where no one knows... I'm sane.......

STRAY

I'm in prison... By my own choosing
I created this wall... Of self-confinement

I didn't have to commit a crime
To be sent to prison
I took life... One day at a time
There was no future... I lived
In increments... Of twenty-four hours

I never thought about your feelings
Being home alone... In a house for two
I was afraid to internalize
What I was doing... Avoiding... Feeling

Guilt... For the lies I told you
Overwhelmed... By being a parent
Ashamed... Of my deceitful life
Lonely... Because of self-pity

I accepted my internal feelings
As positive insecurities... And I felt
Excited... Happy... Confident... Normal
When I didn't have to deal with my situation

I lived life... One beer at a time
In increments of self-denial
Irritated... For not having the courage
To adequately address my internal emotions
I was sentenced to life... Within my own prison.......

SNAFU

We lived in a Spanish style colonial house
With palm trees... That became a home
For the pigeons
On a dirt road... With no name
Surrounded by an orange orchard... That was dying

I walked to school each morning
Took a shortcut across the McBrides' yard
Threw rocks and kicked dirt on my way
School would be my escape

In the second grade you always wanted to be
In the sixth grade
They hung out in the eucalyptus trees
On the playground
And smoked cigarettes and told dirty jokes
Wore Levis and white t-shirts with greased back hair

I heard about the fight
That was to take place after school
Two tough guys would meet in a circle... With pipes
I didn't know what to expect... But I wanted to watch
Pipes hit targets... They fell... Stood up... Fell
Stood up... No more... It was quiet
I was the last to leave
The eucalyptus trees and the school
Lost their meaning to me.......

DIVISIVE

Next to Felicita School
The old tree wouldn't die
It was a testimony
To a tragic event

My tia Ana moved into the abandoned corner house
And even though it was small
It had the aura of a haunted mansion
With only one secret to be revealed

My tia's kids were always being disciplined
My tio was from a different war
One that never existed... In history
He was feared by his gait... And his crooked smile

I don't remember learning why
That old man in the corner house... Hung himself
On that old tree... His knees
Were touching the ground
As the sun was setting... And in the distance
You could hear a dog howl... And the sirens.......

THIEF

The tunas are red... Ripe
They tease me... Tempt me
Make the journey... Solo
Introduce your familia... To the fruit... Of strength

The heat is my ally... Not my foe
The mountain is steep... For an eight-year-old
It is covered with sage... With no route
But I remember a path... Maybe... From a dream

With age... The nopales have become brittle
Like my abuelito who still drinks... Tequila
Even at the age of ninety... It helps with his pain
From his life... Not the disease... That is killing him

As I clutch the tunas in my hands
The espinas... Become beautiful feathers
And I race down the mountain with a pounding heart
To share the fruit of strength... With my familia.......

FEIGN

We were supposed to avoid the creek
My familia told us stories about the Llorona
The woman who drowned her children
So she could be free... From the burden
Of motherhood

She was exiled into misery
Would only appear at twilight
In search of her children
Her tears were the foam... That encased the rocks
That would entice children... Like a bubble bath

I never saw her appear... Or heard her sing
But I swear... If I stayed out to late
I could feel her bony fingers... Caress me
And I wanted to run away... But it was a game
Not to run... When you stayed out... Too late

We lived next to Elfin Forest
It was always eerie and quiet
You never went out after dark... If you were smart
Even the cows and chickens were petrified
Of the loneliness... The darkness... The Llorona.......

INITIATE

In the beginning
There was only darkness
And in that darkness
There was Thought
The only... Existence

Thought... Created Reason
For it knew... That Wickedness
Was starting to form
And create... Another... Existence

Reason... Looked into the future
And saw Wickedness in all its evil
Smelt death... For no purpose
And consciousness was born
To sow the seeds of wisdom

In time... Thought was alone
For Reason was in charge
To give Wickedness a Conscious
To do battle... With the self.......

DIVULGE

I look at things I can't buy
Poor and broke... Cockroaches leave me alone
My toes are cold... As they protrude
Through holes in my existence

I was born under the sign
Of a clone star
So... What should I expect?
Besides a life of uncertainty

I see my wife... Smile
Her grace is unmatched
And I lay my jacket
In puddles of tears

I wake to a fast-beating heart
As sweat is dripping... Inside of my coffin
I have nothing pending
So... I invite death to dinner

I was born under the sign
This is my journey... Unforgiving
I lose reality... To ephemeral beings
And nothing is real... Anymore......

LAW

The quilt is removed
To reveal the landscape below
The world is singing with awakening
And with a pleasant smile
The Sun enjoys the music

The flowers rejoice
And unfold their petals
Releasing a fragrance of enticement
To capture... The Sun

The stream is quiet
On its journey of Reason
The story was told
When the Sun was young

The flowers drink from the stream
And hear the story of Reason
They know that to trap the Sun
Is to leave the Moon alone
And to unbalance... The world.......

DENY

It's so easy... To say those words
We continue to be commodity
The future for people... We have never met
But... Ensure their place in history

We adapt to acceptance
Take that walk back to this
Some push forward... Persevere
Some regress... Quit on themselves

I want to believe... In purpose
That denial is part of life
And growth starts at any age
And the words denied... Are actually hard to say

I understand... That I'm only commodity
When I quit on myself
And don't prepare... For the future
To ensure my place... In history.......

THITHER

Great Grandfather
Help me with this war
That is raging inside of my Heart
I have trouble understanding
The meaning of my Vision

I'm in search of my other
That was stolen from my people
During the war of the conquest
Before I was born

I hunger for knowledge
For peace within my Heart
I sing a song from my Vision
Of a time when my people Danced
Hunted the Buffalo... Deer... Rabbit
And drank from the stream
From melted snow

I burn sage to cleanse my Being
To help me put an end to this war
That is ragging in my Heart
Great Grandfather
Hear my Heart... Give me Courage
To free my Spirit... When the sun is setting
And the wind blows... For the last time......

EPOCH

It starts at dawn
With fresh air
Mixed with morning noise
People regrouping their senses

Dreaming of my last thoughts
The vision I have constructed
The essence of your beauty
That cradles my somberness

I touch the cold concrete floor
Change the radio station
Submerge my face
In cold awakening awareness

I leave your sleeping beauty
In the memory of my darkness
I move about in the light
Talk with your image... Alone

It starts again as night overtakes day
With the moon guiding the way
I see your picture transform
Enliven... My passage... Into night.......

PRINCIPLE

The Beautiful Moon
With her child close by
Surrounded by the darkness
Keeps vigil... As we dream

The coyote howls
In the desert wasteland
He stares at the woman he loves
And he knows... That her husband
The Sun... Is asleep

Each night the coyote
Sings his song
That he learned... As he dreamt
Of the woman he loves

But each night
His song never ends
And the Moon in all her Beauty
Only hears the sounds... Of the world.......

JILL

Blue were the color of her eyes
They were a mirror from the sky
I carried her high school picture with me
It was my morning sunshine

I walked her home after school
Carried her books... Wish I could hold her hand
I loved her accent... Her dimples
When she would smile
But it was those deep blue eyes
That kept me mesmerized

When I look at the blue sky today
I wonder if my eyes were blue
Would she look at the sky
And think about high school
When I would walk her home.......

HIATUS

I wonder if I will remember my name
When I eventually become old
Or will they recognize me and give me a name
From my youth photo?
Or will it matter... Once I'm deceased

I feel the cold make a home on my hands
And my feet laugh inside the comfort of socks
I search for my slippers... No shoelaces
My back is grateful for my consideration

I drag a comb across my hair... Chest
Out of habit... I part it on the side
I turn the lights on... Before I drink my water
Dentures are expensive... And don't go down well

I wonder if my love... Will remember me
Send me kisses and strawberries and poems of love
Or will she become old and also forget
And wonder if I will send her poems of love
With soft kisses... And never forget her name
Once... We become old.......

DISPEL

And so... This is how it begins
One day we're friends... The next
Strangers on a subway
That has no end

Gazing out through the window pane
Life is a blur
Like a fog that won't lift
We move forward into nothingness

Separated by thoughts
That were grown with deception
The tracks of destiny
Are never-ending

And so... This is how it ends
We part ways... Before the end
Of the dream... That was created
Before... We were... Friends.......

DESCENDED

My ancestors are waiting for me
They are gathered around the fire
Taking turns... Telling stories of my life
That hasn't ended in my time

They are growing impatient
Why is it taking so long?
There was only one path to travel
They wonder if I'm talking to the trees

It's a different world
When you were born
To see... To feel... To hear
The sounds of this earth

My ancestors... Will have to wait
Longer for my arrival
Mother Earth is courting me
To be a warrior... Who truly believes
In the magic... Of her seeds.......

FORETELL

I dream
Of my death
The day it will occur
The bullet
That will lay me... To rest

I will lead my warriors
Into battle... I will lead
My dream into death
Death will be my song
That echoes in the valley

Death has come to me
Whispered its message... To set me free
Chanted a song that I will sing
Death... Has honored me

I do not cry
For my departure
I cry for my people
That will stay behind

I ride my will
To the highest hill
I seek the bullet
That will lay me... To rest.......

NECTAR

Your kiss
Was sweet
Like nectar

So... I dream
Remember you
Never shut your eyes

Sweet
My old heart
Savors the nectar

Do you laugh
When you're alone
Remember... It was
Sweet as nectar

I never tired
Of kissing you
You were sweet as nectar

Touching
Made you laugh
Made you young

I'm very old
But remember
Yes... Your kisses
Sweet as nectar.......

PHASE 2

MAKING AMENDS

HONESTY

Accepting my life
As others see it
Not as I perceive it
You were right... I was wrong

I built a wall
On confusion
Answers were evasive
I drank my somberness

Living in denial
Of my addiction
Your love and understanding
Gave my life meaning

My life was unmanageable
I was trapped in the cycle
Of denial... Regret... Self-pity
Until I heard your words... They gave me strength

HOPE

Is having a destination
A point of reference
A beginning and an end
Something to build a future... On

When there is no point of reference
Each day is meaningless to growth
There is nothing to build on
We lose the reason to life... To existence

Externally we adapt
We become part of the fixture
Merge into hopelessness
Feel victimized by circumstances

Internally I have a choice
To break my barriers that were built
On anger... Resentment... Pride
Give life meaning... Direction... With understanding

FAITH

Believing I could be cured
I wasn't alone in my addiction
My addiction had kept me alone
Away from the self... I needed help

I had glimpses... Moving frames
Of my life... When I was sober
They were brief periods
That weren't longer than days

I knew you cared
I heard it in your voice
Saw it in your eyes
My addiction... Wouldn't let me surrender

I hear your words today
They were lyrics to sobriety
I dissolve past the moving frames
I let yesterday... Bring on a new day

DISCIPLINE

That fearless inventory
Revealed the person I was
When I wasn't me
I took life… You… For granted

I suppressed the memories
With laughter… Exercise
I became arrogant
There was no need to search further

I saw a woman cry
Her story was one
But spoke for many
It was emotional… About internal sufferings

Her story wasn't mine…But it was the same
How I inflicted pain… With memories
Scarred your heart… Changed your perception
To live in fear… Because of my alcoholism

COURAGE

It isn't easy to admit
The kind of person I used to be
There is nothing nice... Pleasant
About the harm I caused

I admitted to my Higher Power
To myself... Another Being
About the physical... Emotional
Silent abuse... That was normal

I lived in fear... That communicating
This would reveal my weakness
My love for you... The children
I found courage when I drank

There were brief periods
In my life... When I was sober
I enjoyed your company... Smiled
I became vulnerable... Drank my happiness away

WILLINGNESS

I'm perfect... I'm not defective
I surrender to myself
Who knows me better... Then
Beer... Wine... Whiskey... Pruno

When I'm alone with my thoughts
I remember how I treated
You... Life... Responsibility
I chose immaturity... Not growth

I drove one second from death
I never aged... I was reckless
Out of control... I listened to no one
I was the master of my own destruction

Surrendering the past
Accepting a new future... Way of thinking
I needed help... To find my way
I needed weapons... To battle the self

HUMILITY

I continued my personal inventory
My character still needed maintenance
The realization of not being perfect
Being humble and willing to ask for help

Always falling short of my goals
I never considered even trying
I only saw final results
That kept doubt... Fear... In control of my life

I took the easy way out
Lived in denial... Believed it was meant to be
Always falling short... Would be my motto
I reinforced this thinking... With alcohol

Alcoholics Anonymous is powerful... A true message
From others who needed help... Found meaning
Living sober... Changed their perception of life
Having a goal... Unity... Service... Recovery

COMPASSION

The list never stopped
Each name had a face
Was a human... Had rights
To live... To laugh... To cry

I felt no mercy for my life
It became my attitude
The way I dealt... With people
Morbid... Uncaring... Everything was meaningless

It was difficult to make that list
My pen ran dry... And still there were more
I wanted to quit... Not accept
I was this horrible person

It went beyond death
I was responsible... For your life
For the memories... For futures stolen
Never being the persons... They were born to be

INTEGRITY

My Higher Power gave me strength
To face reality... And make amends
Giving back to society...Humanity
Each day... I live with a different name... Memory

The memories have a face
They had the right to exist
To have a family... Future... Dreams
To play a role in life

I shattered families
Took their future
Created nightmares
I enslaved their life in pain

I live each day making amends
It has become my walk
To give back to society... What I have taken
Healing the hearts... That question life

PERSEVERANCE

To live with myself... Is being calm
Don't overreact... Pause... Relax
Take responsibility... Be accountable
Admit when I'm wrong

Changing who I am... Is a process
There are no days off
No unresolved issues... Lingering thoughts
I live in reality... Not fiction

When I lived in fiction
I put meaning to other person's thoughts
I read between the lines
Used aggressive tactics... To resolve my assumptions

Reality is difficult... Challenging
It's a new way of thinking... Being sober
I understand the rights of others
I continue to strive for understanding

SPIRITUAL AWARENESS

The Spirit has always been my companion
I was left to make my own decisions
I chose a different Higher Power
One that I could taste... Feel... Buy

When I was intoxicated... Drunk
I sought my own Higher Power
Self-gratification... Instant rewards
Status from fake friends

My life was tumultuous
Anger fed my pride... Attitude
I was always ready in my stupor
My thinking was without reason

Three decades later... Talking to the Spirit
Under the comfort of the hot sun
My companion gives me reason to survive
With a new appreciation for life

SELFLESS SERVICE

Leading by example... My words are my walk
Always giving back... I'm no longer powerless
Some days can be overwhelming
They start like yesterday's dreams

The danger that is about to unfold
Has come before... It isn't new... Only suppressed
With this new understanding of my walk
My mind is clear... I'm able to make choices

My alcoholism prevented me from
This understanding... I created scenarios
Far from the truth... I was the only victim...I
Justified my decisions... Lived by deceitful principles

No longer living a nightmare... Always intoxicated
I'm able to give back... In sobriety
I listen... Feel empathy... Have remorse
Every person... Has the right to be free

EVERYDAYNESS

WHO AM I

Am I a Chicano... Mejicano
A vato loco... Lost and confused
Walking the calles... With baggy tramados
Smoking primos... Con mi fantasma

Just yesterday... I was an American
Went to the store... Asked for carne asada
The butcher looked at me... "Que quieres?"
I pointed at the meat... Who am I?

I didn't go to church... Padre forgive me
I pray over my bowl of menudo
No me importa... What they think
Una cerveza... Por favor

I grew up in two worlds
One with frijoles and tortillas
The other with bacon and eggs
Today I wonder... Who am I.......

ONE DAY

To be young again
Just for one day
To remember... What it was like
To enjoy the start of the day

Waking up to the aroma
Of percolating coffee... Before school
The fresh tortillas that my Jefita would make
For my Jefito's lunch
What I would give... For just one day

I'm walking to the bus stop
Smoking before school... I enjoy
The morning breeze and the early sun
Birds playing in the trees

My eyes are tired and my bones ache
I have trouble remembering today
What I would give... For just one day
To be young again... And escape old age.......

ESCONDIDO

Esco-Viejo… Old Escondido
This is how it starts
Orange cones line the streets
It's Friday… The beginning

They park their classic rides
For nostalgia… Remembrance
Of a time past when they were young
Walking on Grand after school

The Ritz is still on the corner
With a new facelift
The once iconic Palomar Hospital
Has given way to a scenic view

This is the end of times
And the beginning
Of a new generation
What memories… Will they leave
Behind……

OBSOLETE

I'm the last storyteller... Recorder of history
Of my people...Before technology
Heard truths and lies from the Elders
Listened to stories of our existence
The way we lived... Survived... Died

We were guided into the future with experience
Firsthand knowledge of what life was
And what it would become

My heart is heavy and my eyes are red
Tears from remembrance
Knowing we have vanished from existence
Gave away our dance and a way of life
To technology

I'm the last storyteller
And soon... I will not exist
My people who I love
Will search for existence
On the internet.......

ORATOR

Making America great again
The statement I've been waiting to hear
This beautiful country
Is going to flourish... With hope

I hear my ancestors cry
See the tears flow down their cheeks
They have waited for this day
Even... In death

We have been deceived before
Built homes on the wasteland
Survived on our will... Not to perish
We refused... To become... Buffalos

I see the Incas... Mayans... Toltecs... Aztecs
They're chanting... Dancing... Giving thanks
We're coming home... Cascading from above
Making America... Great again.......

I'M TRAVELING

I'm traveling into the Spirit World
To give thanks to my Ancestors
Who are no longer here
I hear the beat of drums
They're calling me... To come home

Not to stay... Just to visit
I bring offerings... Stories
How nothing has changed
We're still living in the REZ

My extended family surrounds me
They shape shift into trees
Fly high in the sky as eagles
Turn into a gentle stream

I touch the earth with full awareness
Watch the sun between the clouds
I close my eyes... Hear the drums
They are fading... With time.......

BARE FEET

Bare feet... Walking on dirt
I don't forget where I came from
Father Time is stealing my memories
Of when I was young

I fight this battle... With age
Write down my most precious memories
Recharge my Spirit
Holding you... Next to me
When we were young... Watching the sun

The hours went by too fast
There was no radio... Internet
Only the sounds of the wind
The birds... The creek

It's cold and peaceful today
I take off my shoes
Touch the dirt... Listen to the world
As Father Time stops... And grants me
Another Day.......

U.S. OF A

Will I live long enough
To see Oscar "Zeta" Acosta's
Cockroaches planting maize and jalapenos
In the garden of the Brown House

Who will be the next Pancho Gonzalez
From East Los Angeles to pick up a racket
Go to Wimbledon... Reverse the conquest
Leave the Queen in a state of despair

Who remembers the Mejicano coach
With the Mexican quarterback
Winning the Super Bowl... No mention
Of identity... Tom Flores... Jim Plunkett

Do I cross my arms behind my back
Think of Emiliano Zapata... Dying
On his feet... Not on his knees
I'm proud to be a cockroach ...Living in the
United States of Aztlan.......

HOMELESS

The concrete is cold
My bones ache... I forget who I am
I haven't eaten in three days
Haven't showered since the last rain

My shoes barely conceal my feet
My Levi's are the new fad
Ripped beyond repair
Reflections of my soul

I shiver like a wounded animal
Cup my hands to my lips
Breathe in... Breathe out
Don't let the heat escape

Unwanted by society
I'm a burden to the taxpayer
I build my home on the mountain side
I wait for the destroyers
The taxpayers of this land.......

HELP ME

Help me understand
The meaning of aloneness
I need you by my side
To make this world real

When I think of the past
I have existence
I was born to love my Mother
The Earth

To take care of her children
Nourish them with thoughts
Hear stories of the conquest
How they rode big dogs

Should I put on war paint?
Build a wall… Centuries too late
Maybe I'll dance to my heartbeat
Sweat… Chant… Give thanks
For never forgetting who I am…….

SANTA FE SPRINGS SWAP MEET

The memories are starting to fade away
Like cigarette smoke in my old age
I take a drag and slip away
Let the ashes scatter... When

I used to be that... Cholo
Walking down the calle
Creased down... Strolling hard
Entering your Barrio

Hairnet... Ray Bans... Searching
For what's next... Tagging my placaso
Over your name... As I cross it out
Con safos... Y qui

Today I drink my Modelo Negra
Listen to oldies... Watch the vetranos
Dance to their youth
With their ruca by their side
With dyed hair and red lipstick.......

DREAMS

I keep on having these dreams
Of being chased by the Border Patrol
I am running down the alley
I can almost see my home

I hear the dogs barking
I am sweating and it's cold
I pass by Juanita's Taco Shop
I smell the carnitas on the grill

I hide behind a building that used to be
The Silver Dollar Bar with many memories
I hear the old women and children cry
As Ruben Salazar is shot
And he is dying on the floor

I'm running down the calle
I'm a Chicano marathon runner
Being chased by the Border Patrol
Getting closer to my elusive home.......

MEMORIES

What will you remember about today
Sleeping in the car... Eating menudo
Wanting more birds... Rabbits
Hello Kitty or anything Pink

Or will you remember spending time
With your mom... With me
Never being left alone
Being a family... Protecting each other

Are you nervous?... It's almost time
Quinceanera... Turning into a young lady
Dancing to Karol G "Ocean"... You love your mom
She always has your back

Thank you for being here with us
You are the greatest... From the bottom
Of our hearts... Today we will never forget
Dancing with you... Getting ready
For your quinceanera.......

SUNDAY

I just got out of the Pinta
Spending time with my Jefita
Trying to make up for time lost
Doing things together... Even

If I push you in your wheelchair
I know you have waited for me
Years turned into decades
Your black hair is now gray

We don't speak to each other
We both know our thoughts
The empty space in time
Never existed... You never left

Tomorrow the hummingbird
Might make you smile... Cry
You have waited for me
Waited for my release... And
Now that I am here... You have to leave.......

I'M DYING

I'm dying
These are my last memories
Reliving my youth
I love you... Hold me... Kiss me
Never say goodbye

Does it have to end?
Can't this day last forever?
Me holding you
Looking into your eyes

I have always loved you
Before I was born
I knew I would find you
The woman I would always love

I'm dying... Can I kiss you?
Make you laugh one last time?
Maybe we can dance
Look into each other's eyes... Thank God
For this last chance... At love.......

GLOSSARY

Abuelito	Grandfather
Arroz	Rice, Mexican rice
Aztlan	The mythological land of Aztecs
Barrio	Gang neighborhood
Calle	Street
Carnitas	Pork
Chicano	Mexican person
Cholo	Slang gang member
Con mi fantasmas	With my spirit; ghost; dead person
Con safos	"What's up?" with emphasis; gang challenge
De visitas	Day of visits
Esco Viejo	Old Escondido
Espinas	Cactus thorn; stickers
Familia	Family
Frijoles	Beans
Gente	People
Jefita	Mother
Jefito	Father
La dia	The day
La visita	The visit
Llorona	Mexican folklore; the weeping woman
Loco	Crazy
Maiz	Corn
Mejicano	Mexican
Mi amor	My love
Mija	Affectionate for woman; girl
Nahuatl	Aztec language

No me importa	I don't care
Nopales	Cactus
Pinta	Slang for prison
Placaso	Gang nickname
Por favor	Please
Primos	Slang for marijuana mixed with cocaine; cousins
Que quieres	What do you want?
Quinceanera	Coming of age party for girl on her fifteenth birthday
Raza	Race; ethnicity
Ruca	Girlfriend
Tia	Aunt
Tio	Uncle
Tramados	Slang for pants
Tunas	Cactus apples
Una cerveza	One beer
Vato	Slang for homeboy
Vetranos	Slang for older homeboy

ABOUT THE AUTHOR

Antonio Sinohui Sanchez was born the youngest of six siblings in Santa Clara, California, in March 1960. His family relocated to Escondido, California, where his mother was a housemaid and his father spent time as a migrant farm worker.

By the age of fifteen, Antonio was roaming the streets; in eleventh grade he dropped out of school.

At age twenty, he was arrested for murder and sentenced to fifteen years to life.

Antonio spent the next thirty-six years in the worst penitentiaries in California. Being incarcerated and preparing for multiple parole board hearings took a lot of soul searching and accepting responsibility for the person he was and the person he could become.

Writing helped Antonio reflect on his past and visualize a future after prison. It also played a large part in his finally being granted parole after his eighth time before the board. This book of poems is the beginning of his search to understand his life in the past and present, and hopefully lead a better future.